RICHARD LUNDY

DONEGAL TRAVEL GUIDE 2024-2025

Exploring the Must-See Attractions, Accommodations and Itineraries

Copyright © 2024 by Richard Lundy

All rights reserved. No part of this publication may be reproduced, stored or transmitted in any form or by any means, electronic, mechanical, photocopying, recording, scanning, or otherwise without written permission from the publisher. It is illegal to copy this book, post it to a website, or distribute it by any other means without permission.

Richard Lundy asserts the moral right to be identified as the author of this work.

First edition

*This book was professionally typeset on Reedsy.
Find out more at reedsy.com*

Contents

Introduction	1
About This Guide	1
History of Donegal	2
Chapter 1: Planning Your Trip	4
Best Time to Visit	4
Visa and Entry Requirements	6
Packing Essentials	8
Transportation Options	10
Chapter 2: Must-See Attractions	13
Slieve League (Sliabh Liag)	13
Fanad Head Lighthouse	14
Tory Island	16
Glenveagh National Park and Castle	18
Mount Errigal	19
An Grianán of Aileach	21
Doagh Famine Village	22
Donegal Castle	23
Malin Head	25
Ards Forest Park	26
Chapter 3: Culinary Delights and Cultural Experiences	28
Traditional Donegal Cuisine	28
Top Restaurants and Pubs	30
Cultural Highlights	32
Local Festivals and Events	34
Chapter 4: Beaches and Coastal Adventures	36
Best Beaches in Donegal	36

Coastal Drives	38
Boat Tours and Cruises	39
Chapter 5: Accommodations in Donegal	41
Rental Apartments	41
Hotels and Hostels	44
Chapter 6: Outdoor Activities	50
Hiking and Walking Trails	50
Surfing and Watersports	52
Golf Courses	54
Fishing Spots	56
Cycling Routes	58
Chapter 7: Nightlife in Donegal	61
Bars, Clubs and Live Music Venues	61
Theatres and Performing Arts	63
Chapter 8: Shopping in Donegal	65
Local Markets	65
Souvenir Shops	67
Art and Antique Stores	69
Chapter 9: Planning Your Itinerary	71
A 7-Day General Itinerary	71
A 3-Day Romantic Itinerary for Couples	74
A 5-Day Culinary Itinerary	77
Chapter 10: Practical Information and Tips	81
Language and Communication	81
Currency and Money Matters	83
Health and Safety Tips	85
Conclusion	88

Introduction

About This Guide

Welcome to your ultimate travel companion for exploring County Donegal, Ireland. This thorough guide is your all-in-one resource for planning an unforgettable trip, whether you're a seasoned traveller or visiting the Emerald Isle for the first time.

Inside, you'll find all the information needed to craft a perfect Donegal itinerary. We'll lead you to the must-see attractions, from the breathtaking cliffs of Slieve League to the quaint villages along the coast. History enthusiasts will enjoy our deep dive into Donegal's rich past, exploring its Gaelic origins and historical significance.

Donegal isn't just about stunning landscapes and historical landmarks. This guide will also immerse you in the county's vibrant culture. Savour the flavours of traditional Donegal cuisine and experience the lively pub scene where local music resonates.

Whether you're seeking outdoor adventures or a peaceful retreat, Donegal has something for everyone. We'll provide detailed information on hiking trails, surfing spots, charming towns, and hidden treasures to ensure you make the most of your Donegal experience.

Written to offer clear, concise, and engaging information, this guide aims to be both informative and inspirational. It provides practical details while igniting your wanderlust for this enchanting part of Ireland.

So, lace up your walking shoes, bring your curiosity, and let this guide be your gateway to an unforgettable adventure in County Donegal.

* * *

History of Donegal

County Donegal boasts a rich and intriguing history spanning millennia. Evidence shows that settlements in Donegal date back to the Mesolithic period (around 8000 BC), with early inhabitants likely forming hunter-gatherer communities reliant on the land and sea.

Gaelic Kingdoms and Clans

By the 1st millennium AD, Donegal was entrenched in Gaelic culture, forming part of the powerful kingdom of Tír Chonaill (Tirconnell), under the rule of the O'Donnell dynasty. The O'Donnells, among Ireland's most powerful clans, frequently clashed with the O'Neills for control of Ulster. Donegal Town, the O'Donnells' seat of power, still features the impressive Donegal Castle, a lasting symbol of their influence.

Monastic Influence

In mediaeval times, monasteries were crucial to Donegal's cultural and educational landscape. Religious centres like Donegal Abbey and Doe Abbey became hubs for learning, pilgrimage, and artistic expression, reflecting the era's architectural and artistic achievements.

INTRODUCTION

Turbulent Times

The 16th century saw the arrival of the English, sparking significant upheaval. The Tudor conquest brought rebellions and the eventual decline of Gaelic dominance. A key event was the "Flight of the Earls" in 1607, when the leaders of Tír Chonaill (O'Donnell) and Tyrone (O'Neill) fled Ireland, marking the end of Gaelic rule in the region.

Plantation and Famine

The 17th century introduced English and Scottish settlers, particularly in Inishowen and Laggan, as part of a "plantation" to enforce Protestant control and diminish Gaelic culture. The Great Famine (1845-1852) brought further hardship, devastating Donegal, which heavily relied on potato crops. The Doagh Famine Village offers insight into this tragic period.

20th Century and Beyond

The 20th century witnessed a cultural revival in Donegal, with the Irish language, music, and traditions being actively preserved and celebrated. Today, Donegal is known for its stunning landscapes, rich history, and welcoming spirit, blending ancient ruins with vibrant communities ready to be explored.

Chapter 1: Planning Your Trip

Best Time to Visit

Choosing the best time to visit Donegal depends on your travel preferences and what you hope to experience. Here's a summary of each season's advantages and disadvantages to help you decide:

Summer (June-August)

- Pros: Peak season with the warmest weather and long daylight hours. Ideal for outdoor activities like hiking, cycling, and water sports. Many festivals and events take place.

- Cons: Expect larger crowds and higher prices for accommodation and activities. The weather can be unpredictable with occasional rain showers.

Spring (May & September)

- Pros: These shoulder seasons offer a good balance of decent weather and fewer crowds. Pleasant temperatures for outdoor exploration. Accommodation prices are more reasonable than in peak season.

- Cons: Higher chance of rain compared to summer, and some attractions or tours might have limited hours.

Autumn (October & November)

- Pros: Off-season with minimal crowds and the most affordable accommodation. The scenery features vibrant autumn colours, perfect for nature lovers.

- Cons: Cooler and wetter weather as winter approaches. Shorter daylight hours limit outdoor time. Some attractions or tours may reduce hours or close entirely.

Winter (December-April)

- Pros: Least crowded time with potentially very low accommodation rates. Winter landscapes can be dramatic, especially along the coast.

- Cons: Coldest and wettest weather, with a high chance of rain, wind, and occasional snow. Many outdoor activities are not feasible. Short daylight hours limit exploration time.

Additional Considerations

1. Specific Interests: For surfing or other water sports, summer offers the best conditions. Spring or autumn might be more suitable for hiking and historical exploration.

2. Festivals and Events: Research festivals or events during your travel dates, as they can enhance your trip but may also lead to higher prices and larger crowds.

Ultimately, the best time to visit Donegal is when it aligns with your preferences and priorities. This guide should help you make an informed decision.

* * *

Visa and Entry Requirements

Whether you're a seasoned traveller or a first-time visitor to Ireland, knowing the visa and entry requirements is essential for a smooth start to your Donegal adventure. Here's what you need to know:

Do You Need a Visa?
   Many nationalities don't need a visa for short tourist stays (up to 90 days) in Ireland, including:

1. Citizens of the European Union (EU) and the European Economic Area (EEA) (including Iceland, Norway, and Liechtenstein)

2. Switzerland

3. Citizens of the United Kingdom (UK) - due to the Common Travel Area (CTA) agreement

Travelling from Outside the Visa-Exempt List?
   If your country isn't on the visa-exempt list, you'll likely need to get a visa

before entering Ireland. Here are some resources to help you determine your visa requirements:

1. Irish Department of Foreign Affairs: The official website offers comprehensive information on visa requirements for different nationalities, including an interactive visa checker tool.

2. Nearest Irish Embassy or Consulate: Contact the Irish embassy or consulate in your home country for specific guidance on visa application procedures and required documentation.

General Entry Requirements (For Visa-Exempt Travellers)

Even if you don't need a visa, you'll still need to meet certain entry requirements when arriving in Ireland, such as:

1. Valid Passport: Your passport must be valid for the entire duration of your stay in Ireland (typically for at least six months beyond your departure date).

2. Proof of Onward or Return Travel: Immigration officials may ask for proof that you have a return ticket or onward travel arrangements out of Ireland.

3. Sufficient Funds: Be prepared to demonstrate that you have enough financial resources to support yourself during your stay in Donegal. This could include cash, credit cards, or travel documents with pre-paid accommodation and activities.

* * *

Packing Essentials

The key to a successful trip to Donegal is being prepared for its famously changeable weather. Here's a breakdown of the essentials to ensure you stay comfortable and ready for anything the Emerald Isle throws your way:

Layers

1. Base Layer: Pack thermals (long johns and tops) made from merino wool for excellent moisture-wicking and warmth, even when wet.

2. Mid Layer: Opt for quick-drying fleece or fleece jumpers for additional warmth.

3. Outer Layer: A waterproof and windproof jacket is crucial. Look for breathable materials like Gore-Tex for maximum comfort.

Footwear

1. Hiking Boots: A sturdy pair of waterproof hiking boots will be your best friend for exploring trails and uneven terrain.

2. Walking Shoes: Pack comfortable walking shoes for exploring towns and villages.

Weatherproofing

1. Hat: Bring a warm hat for chilly mornings and evenings. A waterproof hat is ideal for rainy days.

2. Scarves and Gloves: Pack a scarf and gloves for extra warmth, especially if you're visiting during spring or fall.

3. Umbrella: While a compact umbrella can be handy, be prepared for strong coastal winds. A waterproof rain jacket is a more reliable option.

Other Essentials

1. Sunscreen: Don't be fooled by the unpredictable weather! Pack sunscreen with a high SPF for sunny spells.

2. Sunglasses: Sunglasses are a must for those bright, clear days.

3. Refillable Water Bottle: Stay hydrated throughout your adventures with a reusable water bottle.

4. Quick-drying Clothes: A few sets of quick-drying clothes are ideal for activities and easy laundering.

5. Personal Toiletries: Pack all your essentials, including personal toiletries and medications.

Optional Extras

1. Swimsuit: If you plan on visiting beaches or taking boat tours, pack a swimsuit.
2. Adapter Plug: Ensure you have the proper adapter plug for your electronic devices.
3. Daypack: A small backpack is ideal for day trips and carrying essentials while exploring.
4. Hiking Poles: Hiking poles can provide extra stability and support on uneven terrain.

Remember

1. Check the latest weather forecast before packing to tailor your clothing choices accordingly.
2. Pack light and versatile clothing that can be easily layered.
3. Opt for natural fabrics like wool and merino wool for breathability and

comfort.
4. Consider packing a small laundry detergent for quick washes during your trip.

By packing these essentials, you'll be well-equipped to embrace the beauty and adventure that County Donegal has to offer, rain or shine.

* * *

Transportation Options

County Donegal offers various transportation options to suit your travel style and itinerary. Here's a breakdown of the choices available:

Renting a Car

- Flexibility and Freedom: The most popular option, allowing you to explore at your own pace. Scenic coastal roads and charming villages are best experienced with the freedom of a car.

- Availability: Car rentals are readily available at Donegal Airport and in major towns like Letterkenny and Donegal Town.

- Considerations: Driving on the left side of the road may be unfamiliar for some visitors. Be mindful of narrow country roads and the potential for livestock wandering onto the road.

Public Transportation

- Buses: Donegal has a network of public buses operated by TFI Local Link, connecting towns and villages. This budget-friendly option may have less frequent schedules, especially in remote areas.

Taxis

- Convenience: Taxis are available in major towns and are useful for short trips or if you don't want to rent a car. Note that taxis can be expensive for long distances.

Ferry Services

- Scenic Travel: Several ferry services connect Donegal to nearby locations and islands, offering scenic and enjoyable travel options, particularly for day trips to places like Tory Island or Inishowen.

- Popular Routes:
- Rathmullan to Greencastle (Inishowen)
- Burtonport to Arranmore Island
- Maghera to Innisfree

- Information: Ferry schedules and fares are available online for each operator.

Cycling

- Active Travel: Donegal boasts a network of scenic cycling routes. You can rent bicycles in some towns or bring your own for an immersive experience. Be cautious of traffic, especially during peak season.

Walking

- Walker's Paradise: Donegal offers numerous well-maintained hiking trails and scenic walks, catering to all levels, from challenging climbs to leisurely coastal strolls.

Additional Tips

1. Plan Ahead: Plan your route in advance, especially if travelling to remote areas.
2. Travel Passes: Consider purchasing a visitor travel pass for discounted travel on public transportation.
3. Parking: Be aware of limited parking options in some towns, particularly during peak season.

Chapter 2: Must-See Attractions

Slieve League (Sliabh Liag)

Slieve League, known in Irish as Sliabh Liag ("mountain of stone pillars"), is a must-see in County Donegal. Often compared to the Cliffs of Moher, these cliffs are among Europe's most dramatic and tallest, soaring over 600 metres (1,972 ft) at Bunglas Point.

Here's what awaits you at Slieve League:

Stunning Views

The main attraction is the sweeping panorama. On a clear day, you can see the vast Atlantic Ocean, the distant Sligo Mountains, and Donegal's rugged coastline from the viewing platform. Witness the raw power of the ocean waves crashing against the cliffs and the endless Atlantic horizon.

Hiking Trails

Adventure seekers will enjoy the network of hiking trails at Slieve League. The most popular is the One Man's Pass, a looped trail along the cliff edge offering even more spectacular views. This hike is moderately challenging, so wear proper footwear and be prepared for uneven terrain and potential wind gusts.

Pilgrimage Site

The Slieve League has been a pilgrimage site for centuries, with pilgrims climbing the mountain for religious reasons. You can still see parts of the old pilgrim path leading to the summit.

Cultural Significance

The cliffs are rich in local folklore and legends. Ask locals about the mythical creatures and daring rescues tied to Slieve League.

Visitor Center

The Slieve League Cliffs Centre offers extensive information on the area's geology, history, and wildlife. It features exhibits, restrooms, and a cafe.

Things to Consider

1. Wear sturdy shoes with good grip for the uneven terrain.
2. Dress appropriately for variable weather, including wind and rain.
3. Be cautious of strong winds at the cliff edge, especially near the viewing platform.
4. If you plan to hike the One Man's Pass trail, ensure you're in good physical condition and allow enough time to complete the loop.

* * *

Fanad Head Lighthouse

Standing guard on the striking Fanad Peninsula, Fanad Head Lighthouse serves both as an essential navigational tool and a fascinating tourist spot in County Donegal. Constructed in 1817 after the tragic wreck of the HMS

Saldanha in Lough Swilly, Fanad Head Lighthouse has been pivotal in ensuring the safety of maritime traffic along the perilous Donegal coastline.

The lighthouse, designed by esteemed civil engineer George Halpin, features a distinctive 22-metre tall octagonal tower.

Initially, it emitted a fixed white light towards Lough Swilly and a red light seaward, visible up to 14 miles in clear conditions. It switched to electric operation in 1975 and was fully automated by 1983.

Exploring the Lighthouse

Today, visitors to Fanad Head Lighthouse can enjoy various experiences:

1. Guided Tours: Take an intriguing tour with knowledgeable guides who will share the lighthouse's history, its mechanics, and the stories of the lighthouse keepers.

2. Breathtaking Views: Ascend to the top of the lighthouse (if physically able) for sweeping views of the wild Atlantic Ocean, the impressive cliffs of the Fanad Peninsula, and the peaceful waters of Lough Swilly.

3. Visitor Centre: Discover more about the history of Irish lighthouses and their crucial role in navigation. The centre features exhibits on the lighthouse's technology and the challenging yet fulfilling life of lighthouse keepers.

Beyond the Lighthouse

A trip to Fanad Head Lighthouse pairs well with exploring the stunning Fanad Peninsula.

1. Coffee Shop and Craft Shop: Enjoy a drink and a light snack at the on-site coffee shop, and browse through locally-crafted souvenirs at the gift shop to take home a unique memento.

2. Accommodation: For an immersive experience, consider staying in one of the charming former lighthouse keeper's cottages nearby. Imagine waking

up to stunning ocean views and the refreshing sea air.

Planning Your Visit

Fanad Head Lighthouse is open to the public during specific hours, typically in spring, summer, and early fall. Check their website. Guided tours are highly recommended and may need to be booked in advance, especially during peak season.

* * *

Tory Island

Tory Island, known as Toraigh in Irish, is a must-see destination for anyone seeking a unique and unforgettable experience in Donegal. Situated 14.5 kilometres off the northwest coast, it is Ireland's most remote inhabited island.

Tory Island offers a glimpse into traditional Irish life, where Gaelic (Irish language) is predominantly spoken. The island's rich cultural identity shines through its music, storytelling, and artistic traditions.

Visitors are welcomed by the King of Tory, a centuries-old tradition, currently held by artist Patsaí Dan Mac Ruairí. The island features a dramatic landscape with towering cliffs, wild Atlantic scenery, and secluded coves. Hike to Cnoc an Tobair (Hill of the Well) for stunning panoramic views.

Exploring the Island

- Tory Island Loop Walk: This gentle hike covers many key sights, including the ruins of a 6th-century monastery founded by St. Colmcille, a round tower that once sheltered residents from Viking raids, and the Tau Cross, an ancient standing stone.

- An Chlaidze (The Sword): A striking natural rock formation, perfect for photos and offering breathtaking views of the Atlantic.

- Island Crafts and Culture: Explore local shops and galleries showcasing islanders' artistic talents, from traditional knitwear to paintings inspired by the island's scenery, ensuring unique souvenirs.

- Traditional Music Sessions: In the evenings, visit a local pub to immerse yourself in the vibrant music scene. Enjoy a pint while listening to the uilleann pipes, fiddles, and bodhráns.

Planning Your Visit

1. Ferry Services: Daily ferries operate from Maghera Port in County Donegal to Tory Island. Check weather conditions and ferry schedules in advance, as sailings can be affected by rough seas.

2. Accommodation: Options on Tory Island are limited, so book your stay well in advance, especially during peak season.

3. Packing Tips: Prepare for changeable weather, as the island can experience sunshine, rain, and wind all in one day. Sturdy shoes are recommended for exploring the rocky terrain.

***

Glenveagh National Park and Castle

Nestled in the rugged Derryveagh Mountains, Glenveagh National Park and Castle is a jewel in County Donegal's crown. Spanning over 40,000 acres of unspoiled wilderness, dramatic landscapes, and a fascinating castle, Glenveagh offers a glimpse into Ireland's natural beauty and rich history.

At the heart of the park lies Lough Veagh, a sparkling glacial lake encircled by rolling hills, towering mountains, and ancient oak woodlands. Watch for herds of red deer roaming freely, a majestic sight set against the rugged backdrop. Glenveagh offers various walking trails for all abilities. Hike to the summit of Glenveagh Mountain for stunning panoramic views or take a leisurely stroll through the tranquil Victorian walled gardens.

Glenveagh Castle

A splendid example of Scottish Baronial architecture, Glenveagh Castle stands overlooking Lough Veagh. Built in the late 19th century by Captain John George Adair, the castle has a fascinating history. Explore its opulent interiors, adorned with Victorian furniture, artwork, and artefacts. Guided tours reveal the lives of the castle's former residents and the intriguing history of Glenveagh.

Things to Do and See

1. Victorian Walled Gardens: Wander through a haven of colourful blooms and meticulously manicured lawns.

2. Visitor Center: Learn about the park's ecology and conservation efforts.

3. On-Site Cafe: Enjoy a delicious meal or refreshments with stunning views

of the park.

Planning Your Visit

1. Opening Hours: Glenveagh National Park is open year-round, with extended hours during the summer months.

2. Entrance Fees: Fees apply for both park entry and castle tours.

3. Transportation: Public transportation options are limited, so renting a car is recommended. Alternatively, join an organised tour that includes transportation.

* * *

Mount Errigal

Towering above the surrounding landscape, Mount Errigal is a must-visit attraction in County Donegal. Known as the "King of the Donegal Mountains," Errigal is the highest peak in the Derryveagh Mountains, standing at 751 metres (2,464 feet).

It's part of the "Seven Sisters" mountain range, a local term for the series of peaks that dominate the area. The mountain is famed for its distinct pyramid shape and quartzite slopes that glow with a pinkish hue during sunset.

Hiking Mount Errigal

Mount Errigal offers a challenging but rewarding hike for seasoned walkers. The main trail begins near the car park at the base of the mountain. The hike starts on a well-defined gravel path that winds through boggy terrain, making sturdy hiking boots a necessity. As you climb, the trail becomes steeper and rockier, with loose scree (loose stones) requiring careful footing. The final ascent involves a narrow ridge known as "One Man's Path," which requires a good head for heights and can be crowded during peak season.

Things to Consider

1. The hike to Errigal's summit typically takes around 2-3 hours round trip, depending on fitness level.
2. Prepare for variable weather conditions. The summit can be windy and rainy, so pack suitable clothing and rain gear.
3. Bring plenty of water and snacks, as there are no shops or facilities on the mountain.
4. Start your hike early, especially during peak season (May-August), as parking fills up quickly.

Reaching the summit of Mount Errigal offers breathtaking panoramic views of the surrounding landscape, including the Derryveagh Mountains, the Atlantic coast, and even neighbouring counties. The sense of achievement after conquering this iconic peak is immensely rewarding.

If a challenging hike isn't for you, consider these alternatives to experience Mount Errigal's beauty: Take a scenic drive along the N56 road, which provides stunning views of the mountain from a distance. Enjoy a leisurely walk or bike ride on the lower slopes, exploring the surrounding countryside.

Mount Errigal is a symbol of County Donegal's rugged beauty. Whether you hike to the summit or admire it from afar, this iconic peak is sure to leave a lasting impression.

* * *

An Grianán of Aileach

Perched majestically atop Greenan Mountain in Inishowen, County Donegal, the formidable ringfort of An Grianán of Aileach (or Grianán Ailigh in Irish), also known as Greenan Ely or Greenan Fort, commands attention. This ancient structure is a captivating piece of Irish history, offering breathtaking views and a glimpse into the lives of its ancient inhabitants.

History and Legend

The origins of An Grianán of Aileach remain somewhat mysterious, with archaeological findings suggesting occupation dating back to 1700 BC. Attributed to the Northern Uí Néill, a prominent Gaelic dynasty, the fort is thought to have been erected around the 6th or 7th century AD. It served as a significant royal seat for the Kingdom of Aileach, one of Ireland's major Gaelic kingdoms. Steeped in Irish mythology, legends link An Grianán of Aileach to the Tuatha de Danann, a pre-Christian supernatural race. According to folklore, it was constructed by the Dagda, the God-King of the Tuatha de Danann, as a burial site for his son.

Architectural Marvel

An Grianán of Aileach exemplifies a classic dry-stone ringfort, constructed without mortar. Its impressive circular stone wall stands roughly 5 metres (16 feet) high with a diameter of 23 metres (75 feet). Internally, the fort features three terraces where wooden structures likely once stood, providing living quarters. Remnants of these structures offer insights into the lives of the fort's ancient occupants.

Positioned on Greenan Mountain, the fort offers unparalleled views of Donegal. On clear days, visitors can admire the sparkling waters of Lough Foyle and Lough Swilly, with vistas stretching across the vast expanse of the Inishowen peninsula and beyond.

The fort welcomes visitors year-round, with a visitor centre providing interpretive displays and historical information. Guided tours offer deeper insights into its significance.

Accessibility note: Reaching the fort involves climbing a steep path. While the views are rewarding, visitors with mobility limitations should consider this factor.

* * *

Doagh Famine Village

Transport yourself back in time and immerse yourself in the resilience of the Irish spirit at Doagh Famine Village, an extraordinary open-air museum in County Donegal. More than just a collection of old buildings, Doagh Famine Village offers a living history experience. Led by costumed guides, you'll journey through meticulously recreated dwellings, tracing the life and struggles of a Donegal family from the 18th century potato famine era to the present day.

Life in the Famine Era

Experience the harsh realities of the Great Famine firsthand. Explore a traditional thatched cottage, a common dwelling during this time. Learn about the meagre food sources, the devastation of the potato blight, and the fight for survival.

Beyond the Famine

Doagh Famine Village delves into the evolution of rural life in Ireland. Discover how families adapted to changing times, from new technologies to social and economic shifts in the 20th century.

The village encompasses more than just homes. Visit a replica hedge school, a hidden form of education during the Penal Laws era. See a traditional Mass Rock, a clandestine place of worship for Catholics during religious persecution. Guides bring history to life with storytelling and demonstrations, offering a taste of "poteen," a traditional Irish spirit (for the adventurous!).

Relax at the charming cafe with stunning Atlantic coast views. Enjoy tea, coffee, and traditional scones or cakes. Browse the gift shop for unique souvenirs and locally crafted items.

Planning Your Visit

Doagh Famine Village welcomes visitors year-round with regular guided tours. Reasonable admission fees include the guided tour, a complimentary beverage and snack, and possibly a taste of poteen!

* * *

Donegal Castle

In the heart of Donegal Town, Donegal Castle stands as a captivating testament to the region's vibrant history. Constructed in the 15th century by the formidable O'Donnell clan, the castle served as their stronghold and the seat of authority for the Gaelic kingdom of Tír Chonaill.

As one of Ireland's most influential Gaelic families, the O'Donnells wielded significant power, with the castle symbolising their dominance over the area.

Architectural Fusion

Donegal Castle boasts a unique architectural blend. Its core is a rectangular 15th-century keep, a hallmark of Gaelic castles.

In the 17th century, under new English ownership by Sir Basil Brooke, a Jacobean-style wing was added. This addition featured a more ornate facade and spacious rooms, reflecting the evolving dynamics of Donegal and its transition from Gaelic to English rule.

Today, Donegal Castle stands partially restored, offering visitors a captivating glimpse into its storied past. Explore the formidable keep with its stout walls and winding passageways, imagining life within its confines centuries ago. The Jacobean wing hosts an engaging exhibition that delves into the castle's history and its diverse inhabitants. Information panels and guided tours (available during peak season) illuminate the legacy of the O'Donnells, the impact of English influence, and daily life within the castle's walls.

Intriguing Legends

No visit to Donegal Castle is complete without encountering its fascinating legends. One tale suggests that Red Hugh O'Donnell, the last Gaelic chieftain of Tír Chonaill, set fire to the castle himself rather than let it fall to English control. Explore the castle and ponder the truth behind this captivating legend.

For those intrigued by Irish history and mediaeval architecture, Donegal Castle is an essential stop. It offers an immersive experience, transporting visitors back in time and allowing them to connect with the narratives of yesteryear.

Visitor Information

Donegal Castle welcomes visitors with a reasonable admission fee, while free entry is available on the first Wednesday of each month from April to October.

Opening hours vary by season, so it's advisable to check their website. Guided tours offer a deeper exploration of the castle's history and are highly recommended for a richer experience.

* * *

Malin Head

Malin Head, situated on the Inishowen Peninsula, proudly claims the title of Ireland's northernmost point. Malin Head showcases some of Ireland's most stunning coastal scenery, with towering cliffs plunging into the turbulent Atlantic Ocean, creating a breathtaking panorama. On clear days, you can even catch a glimpse of Scotland's distant outline on the horizon.

Hikers will delight in the well-maintained trails that meander along the cliffs, offering awe-inspiring views and opportunities to spot seabirds like gannets, choughs, and the elusive corncrake. Malin Head's history is deeply intertwined with Ireland's strategic significance. The ruins of Lloyd's Signal Station, perched atop the cliffs, served as a crucial communication link in the 19th century, relaying messages between North America and Europe.

During World War II, Malin Head played a pivotal role in monitoring shipping movements, exemplified by its lookout post, a poignant reminder of its wartime importance.

Malin Head offers a haven for nature enthusiasts, where one can explore fascinating rock formations sculpted over millions of years by wind and waves. Nearby Ballyhillion beach showcases a distinctive raised beach system, highlighting the dynamic interaction between land and sea. Keep an eye out for semi-precious stones like agate and carnelian, which may occasionally be discovered on the beach after storms.

Planning Your Visit

Given its remote location, it's essential to plan accordingly. Pack sturdy walking shoes, weather-appropriate clothing (it can get quite windy!), and provisions as facilities at the headland are limited. The nearest village, Malin, lies approximately 16 kilometres south and offers basic amenities such as cafes, shops, and public toilets. While there's no entrance fee to visit Malin Head, it's crucial to be mindful of grazing livestock in the area and adhere to responsible walking practices.

***

Ards Forest Park

Situated along the tranquil shores of Sheephaven Bay, Ards Forest Park beckons with its enchanting blend of diverse landscapes, storied history, and outdoor adventures. Ards Forest Park showcases a remarkable array of ecosystems within its compact confines. Wander through lush woodlands adorned with conifers and deciduous trees, meander along golden sand dunes, or amble along the rugged coastline where waves crash against the shore. The park's freshwater lakes, like Lough Lilly, provide sanctuary to various bird species, while its saltwater counterparts teem with marine life. This rich diversity creates a visually stunning and ecologically vibrant environment.

History enthusiasts will delight in uncovering the remnants of ancient settlements scattered throughout the park. Discover the vestiges of four ring forts, once bastions of defence for Gaelic clans. Explore megalithic tombs, silent witnesses to the region's ancient inhabitants.

Activities for All

Ards Forest Park caters to a wide range of interests. Traverse well-marked trails on foot or by bike, offering options for leisurely family strolls or challenging hikes boasting panoramic coastal vistas. Families will appreciate the designated playground, ideal for keeping young adventurers entertained. Picnic areas with scenic vistas beckon for al fresco dining, while the on-site cafe offers a respite for refreshments.

Nature enthusiasts can indulge in birdwatching, spotting a myriad of avian species from woodlands to cliffs. Keep a lookout for resident red deer and other wildlife that call the park home. A designated hide at the salt marsh trail's end provides a prime vantage point for observing wintering birds as they flock to the marshland ecosystem.

Planning Your Visit

1. Managed by Coillte, Ireland's forestry service, Ards Forest Park requires a small entry fee to help maintain its splendour and amenities.
2. The park welcomes visitors year-round, although some trails may close during inclement weather.
3. Ample parking facilities ensure easy access for visitors arriving by car.
4. Ensure comfortable footwear for navigating uneven terrain, and pack sunscreen, rain gear, and insect repellent based on the forecast.

Chapter 3: Culinary Delights and Cultural Experiences

Traditional Donegal Cuisine

County Donegal boasts a distinct and delicious food culture, influenced by its abundance of fresh seafood, locally grown produce, and long-standing culinary traditions. Here's a peek into the mouthwatering world of Donegal cuisine, along with some suggestions on where to savour it.

Delightful Donegal Delicacies

1. Seafood: Fresh catches from the Atlantic Ocean are at the heart of Donegal's culinary offerings. Enjoy delectable oysters, juicy mussels, or perfectly prepared whitefish. Be sure to try "dulse," a savoury edible seaweed often used in dishes or enjoyed on its own.

2. Hearty Stews and Chowders: Warm up with hearty stews and creamy chowders, a staple of Donegal comfort food. Dive into a bowl of traditional "Irish Stew," featuring tender lamb, potatoes, carrots, and onions, readily available in pubs and eateries. Seafood chowders, brimming with fresh fish and shellfish in a velvety broth, are another beloved option. Prices typically range from €12 to €18 for a generous serving.

3. Donegal Lamb: Celebrated for its delicate taste, Donegal lamb takes centre

stage in local cuisine. Whether roasted with vegetables, simmered in a stew, or presented as a signature dish like "rack of lamb," the flavours are sure to impress. Prices for lamb dishes vary from €18 to €25, depending on the preparation and cut.

4. Potato Creations: The versatile potato holds a special place in Donegal's gastronomy. Try "boxty," a savoury potato pancake made with grated raw and mashed potatoes, often served with butter or fillings. Another favourite is "champ," creamy mashed potatoes blended with scallions and butter. These classic side dishes typically cost between €4 and €6.

5. Baked Delights: Treat yourself to Donegal's array of baked goods, from traditional Irish soda bread to decadent fruitcakes. Don't miss the wholesome "oatmeal bread," perfect for breakfast or a snack. Prices for baked goods range from €2 to €4.

Where to Indulge in Donegal Fare

1. Traditional Pubs: For an authentic dining experience, visit a local pub where hearty stews, chowders, and seafood dishes are served in a lively atmosphere at reasonable prices.

2. Gastropubs: These upscale pubs offer a modern take on traditional fare, using locally sourced ingredients and inventive cooking methods. Expect a refined ambiance and slightly higher prices, typically €20 to €30 for main courses.

3. Restaurants: Whether it's a cosy family-run eatery or an elegant fine dining establishment, Donegal boasts a diverse range of restaurants serving up classic cuisine. Prices vary based on the venue and level of formality.

Additional Suggestions

1. Look for establishments highlighting "locally sourced" or "seasonal"

ingredients on their menus for a taste of Donegal's culinary freshness.
2. Consider opting for a "tasting menu" at a gastropub to sample a variety of Donegal specialties in one sitting.
3. Don't forget to pair your meal with a pint of Guinness or a local craft beer to enhance the flavours and complete the experience.

* * *

Top Restaurants and Pubs

Donegal's culinary landscape is a vibrant blend of fresh, local ingredients and classic dishes infused with contemporary flair. Whether you're seeking a Michelin-recommended dining experience or a cosy pub setting, the county caters to every palate. Here are some standout options to whet your appetite, but don't hesitate to venture off the beaten path and uncover hidden culinary treasures.

Discovering Your Ideal Dining Destination

Please note: Operating hours may vary, especially for pubs with flexible schedules. However, this list offers a helpful starting point for planning your culinary adventures.

1. The Olde Castle Bar & Restaurant, Donegal Town: (Open for lunch from Noon to 8 pm) Nestled near Donegal Castle, this historic gem serves up authentic local fare. Delight in their famed seafood chowder or locally sourced steaks amidst the cosy ambiance of the traditional pub setting.

2. The Narrow Quarter Bistro and Coffee House, Donegal Town: (Generally

open from 9 am to late) This quaint establishment caters to all tastes, offering breakfast, lunch, and creative dinner options featuring fresh, seasonal ingredients.

3. Quay West Restaurant, Donegal Town: (Dinner service typically starts from 5 pm) Enjoy breathtaking views of Donegal Bay while savouring exquisite seafood, premium steaks, and mouth watering vegetarian dishes. Reservations are recommended, especially during peak times.

4. Roadhouse Bar and Restaurant, County Donegal (Various Locations): (Open from 12 pm to 8 pm daily) A go-to spot for casual dining, Roadhouse serves up classic pub fare like fish and chips, burgers, and hearty stews in a family-friendly atmosphere at reasonable prices.

Traditional Pubs and Live Music

1. Dicey Reilly's, Ballyshannon: (Hours vary, typically open late afternoon until late) Immerse yourself in local culture at this historic pub known for its traditional Irish music sessions and lively atmosphere.

2. The Rusty Oven, Kilcar: (Check website or social media for seasonal hours) Cosy up by the fireplace and enjoy local craft beers and homemade pub favourites, often accompanied by live traditional music performances.

3. Smugglers Creek Inn, Rossnowlagh: (Generally open from noon to late) Take in stunning ocean views while enjoying a pint and a satisfying meal. Keep an eye out for live music events featuring talented local artists.

Remember: This list is just the beginning! With an abundance of dining establishments to explore, Donegal promises a culinary adventure full of delightful surprises and authentic flavours.

***

Cultural Highlights

County Donegal is steeped in a vibrant and resilient culture, firmly rooted in its Gaelic heritage. Here's a glimpse into some of the captivating experiences that will enhance your understanding and appreciation of Donegal's distinct identity.

Gaelic Language and Music

The Irish language, or Gaeilge (Gaelic), remains a significant part of Donegal's cultural fabric, particularly in the Gaeltacht regions. Immerse yourself in the melodious tones of Gaelic by joining a traditional music session in a local pub, where the enchanting sounds of fiddles, uilleann pipes, and bodhráns fill the air. Signs and shops often display information in both English and Gaelic, offering a window into the enduring presence of the language.

Traditional Dance and Storytelling

Donegal boasts a rich tradition of dance and storytelling. Experience the lively rhythms of Irish step dance at local festivals or ceilidhs (pronounced kay-lee), communal gatherings filled with music and dance. In cosy pubs and cultural centres, listen to the captivating tales of seanchaí (pronounced shan-ach-ee), skilled storytellers who keep ancient myths and legends alive.

Festivals and Events

Throughout the year, Donegal buzzes with a diverse array of festivals and events. Immerse yourself in the vibrant energy of the Mary from Dungloe International Arts Festival, a celebration of music, dance, and cultural heritage. Experience the artistic brilliance of the Earagail Arts Festival, which showcases visual arts, theatre, and film across the county. Don't miss the Fleadh Cheoil na hÉireann (All-Ireland Fleadh), a prestigious traditional music festival that draws musicians and enthusiasts from far and wide.

Museums and Cultural Centers

Delve into Donegal's rich history and culture by visiting its museums and cultural centres. The Donegal County Museum in Letterkenny offers a comprehensive glimpse into the region's heritage, spanning from prehistoric times to the present. At the Glenveagh Visitor Centre, explore the intriguing story of Glenveagh Castle and its breathtaking surroundings. Smaller local museums scattered throughout the county shed light on specific aspects of Donegal's cultural identity, such as its fishing heritage and traditional crafts.

Local Crafts and Traditions

Donegal is a haven for traditional crafts, lovingly passed down through generations. Support local artisans by purchasing beautifully crafted Aran sweaters, knitted from sumptuous Donegal wool. Admire the intricate patterns of Donegal tweed, a fabric renowned for its quality and craftsmanship. Keep an eye out for demonstrations of traditional crafts, like basket weaving or stone carving, at local festivals or workshops.

Engaging with the Locals

One of the most enriching aspects of Donegal's culture is its warm and welcoming people. Strike up a conversation in a cosy pub, inquire about local customs, or simply bask in the genuine hospitality that defines Donegal. By connecting with the locals, you'll gain valuable insights into the essence of this extraordinary place.

* * *

Local Festivals and Events

Throughout the year, Donegal buzzes with a kaleidoscope of festivals and events, each offering a unique glimpse into the county's vibrant culture. Here's a curated guide categorised by season to help you plan your visit around these lively celebrations.

Spring (March-May)

1. Donegal Town 550th Celebration (March 15th - December 31st): Commemorate Donegal Town's rich history and culture with a year-long program featuring events, exhibitions, and performances.

2. Sea Sessions Surf & Music Festival (June 21st-23rd): Join the festivities in Bundoran for a weekend of music, surfing, and beach fun with both international and Irish acts.

3. Donegal Summer Festival (June 28th-30th): Enjoy live music on the pier in Donegal Town, showcasing local and national talents across various genres.

4. Earagail Arts Festival (July): Experience the best of Irish and international arts, including visual art, theatre, music, dance, and literature, at various locations across County Donegal.

5. MacGill Summer School (July): Dive into Irish language and culture at Glenties' renowned summer school through classes, lectures, workshops, and music sessions.

6. Burtonport Summer Festival (July): Join the festivities in Burtonport for a week of traditional music, dance, competitions, and family fun. (Check website for updates)

7. Sult Fest (August): Celebrate seaweed's wonders in Inishowen with talks, cookery demos, products, and family activities. (Check website for updates)

Autumn (September-November)

1. Glenties Harvest Fair Festival (September): Celebrate the harvest season with local produce, crafts, food demos, music, and fun fair in Glenties. (Check website for updates)

2. Tuff Inish Adventure Race (September): Test your mettle in kayaking, running, cycling, and navigation amidst Inishowen's stunning landscapes.

Winter (December-February)

Clan Gathering - 70th Anniversary (March 15th - October 28th): Honor Donegal's heritage and connect with your roots through clan gatherings, talks, cultural events, and genealogy workshops.

Chapter 4: Beaches and Coastal Adventures

Best Beaches in Donegal

Donegal's rugged coastline is a treasure trove of stunning beaches, catering to a variety of preferences. Here's a curated guide to some of the best beaches in the area.

For Families

1. Narin/Portnoo Beach: A vast, golden strand near Gweebarra Bay, offering shallow, sheltered waters ideal for safe swimming and paddling. Extensive sand dunes provide ample space for building sandcastles and exploring.

2. Fintra Beach: Close to Killybegs, Fintra Beach boasts soft sand and clear waters, with lifeguards during peak season for added safety. Amenities like cafes and toilets make it convenient for families.

For Water Sports Enthusiasts

1. Rossnowlagh Beach: Renowned as a surfer's paradise, Rossnowlagh Beach features consistent waves suitable for surfers of all levels, with surf schools offering lessons and rentals. Vibrant surf communities and competitions add to the excitement.

2. Marble Hill Beach: Popular among experienced surfers and bodyboarders, Marble Hill offers dramatic cliffs and consistent swells, though less suitable

for swimming due to strong currents.

For Secluded Paradise

1. Maghera Beach and Caves: Accessible via a scenic cliff walk, Maghera Beach offers a secluded cove with golden sand and turquoise waters, along with fascinating caves waiting to be explored.

2. Silver Strand (Malin Beg): A hidden gem in the Gaeltacht area near Glencolmcille, Silver Strand boasts pristine white sand, crystal-clear waters, and breathtaking views, accessible via a scenic walk down stone steps.

For Breathtaking Views

1. Slieve League Cliffs and Beach: While not for swimming due to strong currents, Slieve League offers panoramic views of the wild Atlantic coastline and a crescent of golden sand below, perfect for a scenic stroll.

2. Downings Beach: Situated on the Wild Atlantic Way, Downings Beach offers expansive views of Donegal Bay and a long stretch of golden sand, ideal for leisurely walks.

Additional Tips

1. Always exercise caution when swimming in the Atlantic Ocean, and be aware of lifeguard presence and amenities available at each beach.
2. Pack essentials like sunscreen, swimwear, a towel, and a hat for a day by the sea.

* * *

Coastal Drives

Donegal boasts some of Ireland's most stunning coastlines, perfect for exploring via a scenic coastal drive. Here's a peek into some top routes, each offering breathtaking views, quaint villages, and hidden treasures.

The Wild Atlantic Way

This iconic route spans over 2,500 kilometres along Ireland's west coast, with Donegal showcasing its diverse coastal landscapes. Expect charming villages, dramatic cliffs, and secluded coves. Highlights include Slieve League's towering cliffs, Inishowen's rugged beauty, and the golden sands of Maghera Beach.

The Inishowen 100

A 160-kilometre circular route exploring the entire Inishowen Peninsula, boasting dramatic cliffs, hidden coves, and picturesque fishing villages. Must-see spots include Malin Head, Doe Valley's white sand beaches, and the historic Fort Dunree. Don't miss the quaint village of Doagh with its traditional cottages and lively pubs.

The Donegal Bay Drive

Following the western shore of Donegal Bay, this scenic route showcases sandy beaches, rolling hills, and dramatic cliffs. Highlights include the awe-inspiring Slieve League cliffs, the charming town of Killybegs, and the Glencolmcille Folk Village offering insights into Donegal's heritage.

The Fanad Peninsula Loop

Exploring the rugged coastline of the Fanad Peninsula, this loop drive features the iconic Fanad Head Lighthouse and the surfer's paradise of Ballymagan Beach. Portsalon village offers water sports and scenic walks.

Beyond the Main Routes

For an off-the-beaten-path adventure, explore the winding roads of the

Sliabh Liag Peninsula, the Glenties coastline, or the hidden coves of the Rosses.

Tips for Your Coastal Drive

1. Plan for extra time as you'll be tempted to stop and explore frequently.
2. Be cautious on narrow and winding roads, especially in remote areas.
3. Bring snacks and drinks as amenities may be scarce.
4. Consider using a Wild Atlantic Way map or GPS app for navigation.

* * *

Boat Tours and Cruises

The stunning coastline of County Donegal beckons exploration, with a plethora of boat tours and cruises offering unique perspectives on the Atlantic Ocean. Here's a rundown of the diverse options to elevate your Donegal adventure.

Cliff Coast Cruises

Experience the grandeur of Slieve League or Sliabh Liag, Europe's highest accessible sea cliffs, as you cruise beneath their towering heights. Keep an eye out for nesting seabirds like puffins and guillemots. Recommended operators include Atlantic Coastal Cruises in Killybegs and Sliabh Liag Boat Tours at Teelin Pier.

Island Hopping Adventures

Delve into the hidden treasures of Donegal's islands, from the artistic heritage of Tory Island to the unique landscapes of Inishowen. Explore Gaelic culture and traditional craftsmanship on a day trip or cruise. Tory Island Day

Trips from Bunbeg and Inishowen Island Tours offer immersive experiences.

Wildlife Watching Cruises

For nature lovers, wildlife watching cruises provide opportunities to spot dolphins, whales, and basking sharks off the Donegal coast. Knowledgeable guides enhance the experience with insights into marine life. Recommended operators include Whale and Dolphin Watching West in West Donegal and Tory Island Boat Tours (seasonal).

Scenic Day Cruises

Relax and soak in the beauty of Donegal Bay on a scenic day cruise. Admire historical landmarks like Donegal Castle and coastal lighthouses while enjoying panoramic views. Consider Donegal Bay Waterbus departures from Donegal Town Pier or explore options from coastal towns like Killybegs and Burtonport.

Additional Considerations

1. Choose a tour based on duration, itinerary, and desired experience.
2. Check weather conditions and book in advance, especially during peak seasons.
3. Dress appropriately with layers and waterproof gear, and don't forget sun protection.

Chapter 5: Accommodations in Donegal

Rental Apartments

These apartments provide a range of options from central town locations to peaceful countryside retreats, ensuring a comfortable stay for every visitor to Donegal.

1. The Loft, Killybegs: Located above a seafood restaurant, this apartment offers stunning harbour views and easy access to bars and restaurants. It includes a fully equipped kitchen, WiFi, and free parking.

- Location: Main Street, Killybegs
- Price: Around €150 per night

2. Upper Apartment @ Buttermilk: A modern apartment with beautiful views, featuring a fully equipped kitchen, WiFi, and parking. Ideal for couples or small families.

- Location: Portnablagh
- Price: Approximately €140 per night

3. Ann's Country Apartment: Set on a hill with sea views, this apartment

includes a private entrance, kitchen, WiFi, and ample parking. It's perfect for a peaceful countryside stay.

- Location: Killybegs
- Price: Around €130 per night

4. The Lodge Donegal Town: This modern apartment features a fully equipped kitchen, WiFi, and free parking. It's located close to Donegal Town's amenities.

- Location: Donegal Town
- Price: Approximately €160 per night

5. Robin's Nest: A spacious apartment with a kitchen, WiFi, and parking. Guests can enjoy mountain views and easy access to local attractions.

- Location: Donegal
- Price: Around €150 per night

6. The BaaHouse Suite: Featuring modern amenities such as a kitchen, WiFi, and free parking, this suite offers a comfortable stay with scenic views.

- Location: Near The Balor Theatre
- Price: Approximately €170 per night

7. Barnes Escape: A small, fully furnished studio apartment with kitchen facilities, WiFi, and free parking. It is located near popular local pubs and attractions.

- Location: Near Donegal Town

- Price: Around €120 per night

8. G's Barn: This charming apartment offers a cosy atmosphere with modern amenities including a kitchen, WiFi, and parking.

- Location: County Donegal
- Price: Approximately €130 per night

9. Seaview Apartment: Located in Bundoran, this apartment provides sea views, a fully equipped kitchen, WiFi, and free parking. Ideal for beach lovers.

- Location: Bundoran
- Price: Around €140 per night

10. Sailor's View: A well-appointed apartment with a kitchen, WiFi, and parking, offering beautiful sea views. Perfect for a tranquil retreat.

- Location: County Donegal
- Price: Approximately €150 per night

* * *

Hotels and Hostels

These accommodations offer a range of options from luxury hotels to budget-friendly hostels, catering to different tastes and budgets while allowing you to explore the scenic beauty of Donegal

Hotels

1. Harvey's Point: Luxurious hotel known for its breathtaking views of Lough Eske and the Blue Stack Mountains. Renowned for top-tier accommodation and fine dining.

- Location: Shores of Lough Eske, Donegal Town
- Amenities: Free high-speed internet, bicycle rental, free breakfast, business centre, allergy-free rooms.
- Price: From €200 per night

2. Lough Eske Castle: A 5-star castle hotel offering luxurious accommodations in a historic setting.

- Location: Near Lough Eske, Donegal Town
- Amenities: Spa, indoor pool, fine dining restaurant, fitness centre.
- Price: From €250 per night.

3. Rockhill House: A country manor house set on a beautiful estate, known for its elegant rooms and period charm.

- Location: Letterkenny
- Amenities: On-site dining, bars, garden, free Wi-Fi.
- Price: From €150 per night.

4. Redcastle Hotel: A four-star oceanfront resort popular with couples, featuring a luxurious spa.

- Location: Shores of Lough Foyle, Inishowen Peninsula
- Amenities: Spa, pool, sauna, steam room, restaurant and bar.
- Price: From €120 per night.

5. Shandon Hotel & Spa: Overlooking Sheephaven Bay, this hotel offers a perfect mix of relaxation and scenic beauty.

- Location: Near Marble Hill Strand, Dunfanaghy
- Amenities: Thermal spa, relaxation room, outdoor hot tub, family suites.
- Price: From €140 per night.

6. Arnolds Hotel: Family-friendly hotel with views of Sheephaven Bay, close to beaches and hiking trails.

- Location: Dunfanaghy
- Amenities: Restaurant, burger bar, free Wi-Fi.
- Price: From €100 per night.

7. Mill Park Hotel: Modern hotel known for comfort and convenience, close to local attractions.

- Location: Donegal Town
- Amenities: Restaurant, bar, pool, fitness centre.
- Price: From €120 per night.

8. The Central Hotel: Centrally located hotel offering easy access to the town's main attractions.

- Location: Donegal Town
- Amenities: Indoor pool, restaurant, bar, free Wi-Fi.
- Price: From €90 per night.

9. The Abbey Hotel: Historic hotel with a lively atmosphere, situated in the heart of Donegal Town.

- Location: Donegal Town
- Amenities: Restaurant, bar, live entertainment, free Wi-Fi.
- Price: From €80 per night.

10. St. Columbs House: A beautifully renovated period property with charming and characterful rooms.

- Location: Buncrana
- Amenities: Free Wi-Fi, breakfast, garden.
- Price: From €110 per night.

Hostels

1. Errigal Hostel: Part of Hostelling International, set in the Gaeltacht region with access to various outdoor activities.

- Location: Dunlewey, Gweedore
- Amenities: Free Wi-Fi, self-catering kitchen, common area, laundry facilities.
- Price: From €20 per night.

2. Tullyarvan Mill Hostel: Housed in a restored mill, this hostel offers cosy and spacious dormitories.

- Location: Buncrana
- Amenities: Free Wi-Fi, self-catering kitchen, common area.
- Price: From €25 per night.

3. Donegal Town Independent Hostel: Centrally located hostel providing a budget-friendly option for travellers.

- Location: Donegal Town
- Amenities: Free Wi-Fi, kitchen facilities, common room.
- Price: From €18 per night.

4. Sandrock Holiday Hostel: Located at Ireland's most northerly point, ideal for those looking to explore rugged landscapes.

- Location: Malin Head
- Amenities: Free Wi-Fi, kitchen, common room.
- Price: From €20 per night.

5. Malinbeg Hostel: A remote hostel ideal for hiking and exploring Donegal's coastal scenery.

- Location: Glencolumbkille
- Amenities: Kitchen, free parking, common room.
- Price: From €22 per night.

6. The Ritz: Simple and clean hostel in the heart of the fishing town of

Killybegs.

- Location: Killybegs
- Amenities: Free Wi-Fi, self-catering kitchen, common room.
- Price: From €20 per night.

7. Moville Boutique Hostel: Stylish hostel offering a mix of private and dormitory rooms.

- Location: Moville
- Amenities: Free Wi-Fi, garden, kitchen.
- Price: From €25 per night.

8. Ionad Siul: Small hostel perfect for outdoor enthusiasts.

- Location: Dunfanaghy
- Amenities: Kitchen, common area, free Wi-Fi.
- Price: From €22 per night.

9. The Bluestack Centre Hostel: Situated in the Bluestack Mountains, great for hiking.

- Location: Drimarone, Donegal
- Amenities: Free Wi-Fi, kitchen, laundry facilities.
- Price: From €18 per night.

10. Apple Hostel: Budget-friendly hostel in the town centre.

- Location: Letterkenny

CHAPTER 5: ACCOMMODATIONS IN DONEGAL

- Amenities: Free Wi-Fi, kitchen, common area.
- Price: From €20 per night.

Chapter 6: Outdoor Activities

Hiking and Walking Trails

County Donegal is a haven for hikers and walkers, featuring a variety of trails suitable for all skill levels and fitness. From demanding mountain hikes to leisurely coastal walks, Donegal offers a chance to experience its breathtaking scenery on foot.

Mountain Trails

1. Mount Errigal: Reach the highest peak in Donegal (751 metres) for stunning panoramic views. This challenging hike offers vistas of surrounding mountains, valleys, and the Atlantic Ocean.

2. Slieve League (Sliabh Liag): Traverse dramatic cliffs to the pilgrim path and viewing point, providing incredible coastal views and towering sea stacks. This moderate to challenging trail requires good fitness.

3. Muckish Mountain: Take on a challenging yet rewarding hike to the summit of Muckish Mountain (668 metres) for sweeping views of Donegal Bay and nearby peaks. This trail is best for experienced hikers.

Coastal Trails

1. Wild Atlantic Way Walking Trails: Explore segments of the Wild Atlantic Way on foot, enjoying dramatic cliffs, secluded coves, and quaint coastal

villages. Options range from shorter, family-friendly walks to longer, multi-day hikes, including the Slieve League Coastal Walk and the Fanad Head Loop.

2. Donegal Gaeltacht Walk: Experience the scenic beauty of the Gaeltacht (Irish-speaking) region on this coastal route, passing rolling hills, hidden beaches, and traditional Irish cottages.

Moderate Trails

1. Glenveagh National Park: Discover a variety of trails within the park, from gentle forest walks to moderate hikes with views of Lough Veagh and the surrounding mountains. The Garden Trail is a charming choice, showcasing the park's diverse plant life.

2. Ards Forest Park: Hike or bike along well-marked trails through diverse landscapes, including woodlands, sand dunes, and coastal cliffs. Trails cater to all abilities, with shorter family-friendly paths and more challenging hikes with scenic rewards.

Easy Trails

1. Lakeside Walk (Glenveagh National Park): Enjoy a leisurely walk around the picturesque Lough Veagh, spotting wildlife and taking in the park's beauty. This flat, accessible trail is perfect for families and those seeking a relaxing stroll.

2. Riverbank Walk (Donegal Town): Take a scenic walk along the River Erne in Donegal Town. This easy trail offers pleasant views of the town, bridges, and surrounding countryside.

Additional Tips

1. Check weather conditions before heading out and dress in layers with waterproof gear.
2. Wear sturdy footwear with good grip for uneven terrain.

3. Bring plenty of water and snacks.
4. Respect the environment by taking all litter with you.
5. Obtain walking maps or download GPS tracks for unfamiliar trails.

Whether you're an experienced hiker or a casual walker, Donegal's trail network offers a memorable exploration of the county's diverse landscapes and stunning scenery. Lace up your boots, breathe in the fresh air, and uncover the magic of Donegal on foot.

* * *

Surfing and Watersports

County Donegal's rugged coastline and powerful Atlantic waves make it a paradise for surfers and watersports enthusiasts. Whether you're an expert or a beginner, Donegal has something for everyone.

Surfing Paradise

Donegal is home to some of Ireland's most famous surf breaks, drawing surfers from around the globe. Popular spots like Bundoran, Rossnowlagh, Lahinch, and Fintra offer a range of wave types suitable for all skill levels.

- Beginners can start with gentle, rolling waves and learn the basics at surf schools such as:

- Experienced surfers can challenge themselves on more demanding breaks with powerful swells.

Beyond Surfing

Donegal's watersports scene isn't limited to surfing. Here are some other activities to enjoy:

1. Stand-Up Paddleboarding (SUP): Explore the stunning coastline from a unique vantage point. Many surf schools offer SUP rentals and lessons.

2. Kayaking: A fun way to explore hidden coves and secluded beaches. Guided tours let you discover Donegal's marine life and hidden gems, while experienced kayakers can go on their own adventures. Popular operators include:

- Mullaghmore Sea Kayaking in Mullaghmore.

3. Coasteering: For an adrenaline rush, try coasteering, which combines cliff jumping, scrambling, and swimming along the dramatic coastline. Guided tours with experienced operators ensure safety and excitement. Popular coasteering operators include:

- Donegal Adventure Centre in Dunfanaghy

Essential Information

1. Wetsuits are essential due to cool water temperatures year-round. Surf schools usually include wetsuit rentals with their lessons.
2. Safety: Always check weather and surf conditions before heading out. Be aware of tides and currents, and follow the advice of experienced

instructors or guides.

* * *

Golf Courses

County Donegal is a golfer's paradise, featuring championship courses and hidden gems set amidst breathtaking landscapes. Whether you're an experienced player or a casual enthusiast, Donegal offers a course to challenge and inspire. Here's a breakdown of some of the county's most renowned golf courses.

Championship Links

1. Donegal Golf Club (Laghy): Consistently ranked among Ireland's best, this 18-hole links course on the Murvagh Peninsula offers stunning Atlantic Ocean views.

2. Ballyliffin Golf Club (Inishowen): Home to two championship links courses, Glashedy Links and Pollana Strand. Glashedy Links is known for its dramatic cliffside setting, while Pollana Strand provides a more forgiving yet scenic experience.

3. Portsalon Golf Club (Milford): Established in 1891, this historic links course features natural beauty, challenging bunkers, and views of Lough Swilly.

4. Rosapenna Golf Links (Downings): Offers two championship links courses, Sandy Hills Links and St. Patrick's Links. Sandy Hills is perfect for links purists, while St. Patrick's Links offers spectacular ocean views and a more

forgiving layout.

Hidden Gems

1. Narin & Portnoo Links (West Donegal): This 18-hole links course provides stunning views of Narin Beach and the Atlantic Ocean, known for its affordability and friendly atmosphere.

2. Bundoran Golf Club (Bundoran): Established in 1895, this historic parkland course offers mature trees, water hazards, and countryside views.

3. Greencastle Golf Club (Inishowen): This scenic links course features views of Lough Foyle and Greencastle Harbor, known for its challenging layout and friendly atmosphere.

Additional Tips

1. Green Fees: Vary by course, season, and time of day. Booking in advance is recommended, especially during peak season.
2. Equipment Rentals: Most courses offer club rentals for travellers.
3. Etiquette: Familiarise yourself with basic golf course etiquette.
4. Dress Code: Typically requires collared shirts, tailored shorts or trousers, and soft-soled shoes.

From world-class championship links to charming hidden gems, Donegal caters to golfers of all levels. Tee off amidst stunning scenery, enjoy the challenge and camaraderie of the sport, and create lasting memories on your Donegal golfing adventure.

* * *

Fishing Spots

County Donegal is an angler's paradise, with a diverse coastline, numerous freshwater lakes, and rivers teeming with a variety of fish. Here's a guide to some of the most renowned fishing spots in Donegal, categorised by fishing type:

Sea Angling

Shore Fishing

Donegal's dramatic coastline offers excellent opportunities for shore fishing. Popular locations include:

1. Teelin Pier: Deep water access is known for cod, whiting, flatfish, and conger eel.

2. Bloody Foreland to Ardara: Rocky platforms are ideal for catching pollack, mackerel, coalfish, and wrasse.

3. Mulroy Bay: Sheltered waters perfect for small boat fishing, with catches of thornback ray, dogfish, and flatfish.

4. St. John's Point: Known for its deep water and strong currents, ideal for experienced anglers seeking large fish like porbeagle, bluefin tuna, and blue shark.

Boat Fishing

Deep-sea fishing charters offer the chance to catch trophy fish. Popular locations include:

1. Killybegs: A major fishing port with charter boats targeting cod, ling, pollack, and other deep-sea species.

2. Burtonport: Charters operate targeting species like shark, tuna, and marlin (seasonally).

3. Inishowen: Boat trips from Greencastle and other points, targeting a variety of fish depending on the season.

Freshwater Fishing

Donegal boasts numerous freshwater lakes and rivers ideal for fly fishing and coarse fishing. Renowned locations include:

1. The Rosses Fishery: Access to over 130 lakes within a five-mile radius of Dungloe, perfect for fly fishing for brown trout and salmon.

2. Lough Melvin: Known for wild brown trout and salmon fishing. Permits are required.

3. Glenveagh National Park: Offers several lakes stocked with brown trout, providing a scenic backdrop for fishing.

4. Finn and Mourne Rivers: Excellent for salmon and trout fishing, with proper permits required.

Important Information

1. Fishing Licences: A valid fishing licence is required for all anglers over 12 years old in Ireland. Licences can be purchased online or from authorised retailers.

2. Fishing Seasons: Different fish species have specific seasons. Research regulations before heading out to ensure responsible and legal fishing.

3. Local Knowledge: Local tackle shops or experienced anglers can provide valuable insights on the best spots, techniques, and bait depending on the season and target species.

4. Respecting the Environment: Always practise responsible fishing methods, dispose of waste properly, and minimise your impact on delicate ecosystems.

With its diverse fishing opportunities, stunning scenery, and friendly atmosphere, County Donegal is a dream destination for anglers of all skill levels. Cast a line, experience the thrill of the catch, and create lasting memories on your Donegal fishing adventure!

* * *

Cycling Routes

County Donegal is a cyclist's paradise, featuring a network of scenic routes that cater to all levels of experience. From challenging climbs with breathtaking views to leisurely coastal rides, Donegal offers a variety of cycling adventures.

The Wild Atlantic Way
Experience the best of Donegal's coastline on this epic route, part of the larger EuroVelo 1 route that traverses Europe. Stretching from Glencolmcille in South Donegal to Malin Head in the north, this route offers stunning coastal scenery, charming villages, and historical landmarks.

- This route is challenging due to its distance and hilly sections, best suited for experienced cyclists with good fitness levels.

The Donegal Cycle Route
This 200km route is perfect for cyclists seeking scenic and varied terrain. It follows local roads and quiet lanes, connecting towns and villages throughout

the county, and offers stunning mountain views, charming villages, and historical sites.

- Suitable for cyclists with moderate fitness levels as there are some hilly sections.

Greenway Routes

For a more relaxed cycling experience, explore Donegal's growing network of greenways. These converted railway lines offer mostly flat terrain, ideal for families or casual cyclists. Popular greenway routes include:

- The Great Western Greenway (Letterkenny to Derry): Currently under development. Check local tourism websites for updates.

Mountain Biking Adventures

Mountain bike enthusiasts can tackle challenging off-road trails in locations like Glenveagh National Park and Sliabh Liag (Slieve League). These trails offer stunning scenery and a true test of cycling skills. Ensure you have the appropriate equipment and experience.

Additional Tips

1. Helmets: Mandatory for all cyclists under 18 in Ireland. Strongly recommended for all cyclists for safety.
2. Traffic: Be aware of traffic on some roads, especially during peak season.
3. Navigation: Invest in a good quality bike map or cycling app to navigate your chosen routes.
4. Bike Rentals: Many towns and villages offer bike rentals, making it convenient to explore without bringing your own equipment.

Whether you're a seasoned cyclist or a casual rider seeking scenic exploration, Donegal offers a cycling route to suit your preferences. Hop on a bike, breathe in the fresh air, and discover the beauty of Donegal at your own pace.

Chapter 7: Nightlife in Donegal

Bars, Clubs and Live Music Venues

Donegal's nightlife offers a diverse array of experiences, from traditional pubs with lively music to trendy bars with creative cocktails.

Traditional Pubs

At the heart of Donegal's nightlife are its traditional pubs. These cosy spots provide a welcoming atmosphere, friendly locals, and a genuine taste of Irish culture. Live music featuring fiddles, bodhráns, and uilleann pipes adds to the vibrant ambiance.

- Operation Hours: Generally open from noon until late, with some closing earlier on Sundays.
- Entry Fee: Usually free, though there might be a cover charge for special live music events.

Lively Pubs and Gastropubs

These modern pubs, while retaining Irish charm, offer a broader selection of beers, including craft options, and serve tasty pub fare or gastropub menus. Live music ranges from traditional sessions to cover bands and DJs.

- Operation Hours: Similar to traditional pubs, often with extended hours.
- Entry Fee: Typically no entry fee, but there might be charges for specific music events.

Cocktail Bars and Nightclubs

For a more upscale night out, Donegal has cocktail bars and nightclubs with innovative drinks, DJs, and dance floors. These venues attract a trendy crowd.

- Operation Hours: Cocktail bars usually stay open later than pubs, and nightclubs open late and run until the early hours.
- Entry Fee: Some venues may charge an entry fee, particularly on weekends or for special events.

Finding the Perfect Spot

The best way to experience Donegal's nightlife is to explore its streets and visit the pubs and bars that intrigue you. Many towns have clusters of options in central areas.

- Check local tourism websites and apps for live music schedules.
- Ask locals for recommendations to discover favourite spots or hidden gems.

Important Note

Irish pub culture emphasises socialising and conversation. Be considerate of noise levels and avoid disruptive behaviour. Always drink responsibly and have a designated driver if you plan to visit multiple places.

* * *

Theatres and Performing Arts

Donegal's rich cultural landscape extends beyond its traditional pubs and vibrant music scenes. The county is home to a flourishing array of theatres and performing arts venues, showcasing a diverse range of productions year-round.

Key Theatres

1. An Grianán Theatre (Letterkenny): Known as the county's premier venue, An Grianán Theatre hosts a wide range of professional productions, spanning drama, comedy, music, and dance. Its offerings cater to audiences of all ages and interests.

- Operation Hours: The box office is typically open on weekdays from 10:00 AM to 5:00 PM, with evening performances starting around 8:00 PM.
- Entry Fee: Ticket prices vary based on the show. Visit the An Grianán Theatre website for current listings and ticket details.

2. The Balor Arts Centre (Ballybofey): This versatile arts centre presents a diverse array of performances, including theatre, music, dance, and film screenings. It also provides a platform for local and emerging artists, fostering creativity within the community.

- Operation Hours: Box office hours are usually weekdays from 9:00 AM to 5:00 PM, with evening shows beginning around 8:00 PM.
- Entry Fee: Ticket prices vary by event. Check The Balor Arts Centre website for up-to-date listings and ticketing information.

Smaller Venues and Community Theatre

In addition to major theatres, Donegal offers numerous smaller venues and community theatre initiatives. Local pubs often host traditional music sessions featuring talented musicians, while villages and towns may have their own drama societies or theatre groups.

Information about these smaller venues and community productions can be found on local websites, at tourist information centres, or by asking knowledgeable locals.

Tips for Theatre-Goers

1. Book tickets in advance, either online or at the box office, especially for popular shows.
2. Remember that tickets for popular productions tend to sell out fast, so plan accordingly.
3. Dress code at theatres is typically smart casual, though some special events may call for more formal attire.
4. Sit back, relax, and immerse yourself in the artistic offerings of Donegal!

Chapter 8: Shopping in Donegal

Local Markets

County Donegal provides a shopping experience that goes beyond the ordinary high-street stores. Immerse yourself in the lively ambiance of local markets, where you'll stumble upon an array of locally-made crafts, fresh produce, and specialty food items.

Country Markets

A network of Country Markets operates across Donegal, offering an authentic and charming shopping adventure. These markets, run by producers, showcase a diverse range of locally sourced goods. You can expect to find fresh veggies, homemade jams, baked treats, artisanal jewellery, artwork, and more. Each market boasts its own unique vibe and selection of products.

Here are some popular Country Markets along with their operating hours:

1. Carrick Country Market: Old School, Saturdays from 11:00 AM to 1:00 PM.
2. Kilclooney Country Market: The Dolmen Centre, Saturdays from 11:00 AM to 1:00 PM.
3. Ramelton Country Market: Ramelton Town Hall, Saturdays from 11:00 AM to 12:30 PM. (Also in Market Square, Letterkenny, every second Friday from 10:00 AM)
4. Dunfanaghy Country Market: Ozanam Centre, Saturdays from 11:00 AM

to 1:00 PM.
5. Leghowney Country Market: Leghowney Hall (Barnesmore), 2nd & 4th Saturdays of the month from 11:00 AM to 1:00 PM.

Farmer's Markets

Several towns and villages host seasonal farmer's markets, offering an abundance of fresh local produce, artisanal cheeses, homemade bread, and locally-raised meats.

These markets are a wonderful way to support local farmers and savour the flavours of Donegal's fresh bounty.

Craft Markets and Fairs

Throughout the year, Donegal buzzes with various craft markets and fairs, showcasing the talents of local artisans and craftspeople. These events are perfect for finding handcrafted souvenirs and gifts. From knitted sweaters and Donegal tweed to pottery and jewellery, these markets are a treasure trove for unique finds.

For market enthusiasts

1. Carry cash, as some vendors may not accept credit cards.
2. Many markets operate on weekends or specific days, so plan accordingly.
3. Bring reusable shopping bags to reduce waste.
4. Don't hesitate to chat with vendors; they're often passionate about their products and happy to share stories.

While markets offer a concentrated dose of local charm, don't overlook the independent shops and boutiques in Donegal's towns and villages. You'll discover a curated selection of locally-made products, clothing, and souvenirs.

CHAPTER 8: SHOPPING IN DONEGAL

* * *

Souvenir Shops

County Donegal is a haven for souvenir hunters, boasting a delightful array of locally-crafted keepsakes and unique mementos to commemorate your Irish escapade.

Traditional Craft Shops

Scattered throughout towns and villages, these charming shops showcase the talents of local artisans. Discover hand-knitted Aran sweaters, famed for their warmth and intricate designs, crafted from authentic Donegal wool. Peruse handwoven scarves, throws, and blankets featuring traditional patterns. These shops also offer an assortment of other locally-made crafts, such as Connemara marble or silver jewellery, hand-painted pottery, wood carvings, and unique paintings depicting Donegal's landscapes.

- Operation Hours: Typically open from 10:00 AM to 5:30 PM, Monday to Saturday. Some may extend hours during peak tourist seasons (June-August) and close earlier on Sundays (around 4:00 PM) or operate with reduced hours.

Irish Tweed Shops

Donegal's reputation for high-quality tweed precedes it. Explore shops specialising in tweed garments and accessories, ideal for those seeking a touch of Irish heritage and timeless style. From jackets and hats to scarves and homeware items, you'll find an array of pieces crafted from this exquisite fabric.

- Operation Hours: Similar to traditional craft shops, with potential extended hours during peak seasons and reduced hours on Sundays.

Gift Shops

Towns and tourist hubs boast gift shops catering to a wider range of souvenirs. Discover postcards, keychains, magnets, and other trinkets featuring iconic Donegal landmarks or Irish symbols. These shops often stock Irish souvenirs beyond Donegal, like t-shirts with witty slogans or mugs adorned with Celtic designs.

- Operation Hours: Generally open longer hours than traditional craft shops, potentially from 9:00 AM to 6:00 PM, seven days a week. Extended hours are common during peak seasons.

Tips for Souvenir Shopping

1. Look for the "Made in Ireland" logo for authentic crafts.
2. Haggling isn't typical in Irish retail stores; prices are usually fixed.
3. While major credit cards are accepted in many shops, having Euros on hand is convenient for smaller purchases or street vendors.
4. Consider luggage restrictions when choosing souvenirs.
5. Most importantly, enjoy the treasure hunt and bring home a piece of Donegal's enchantment!

* * *

Art and Antique Stores

County Donegal is a haven for art and antique aficionados, offering a delightful array of galleries, studios, and vintage shops brimming with treasures waiting to be discovered.

Art Galleries and Studios

Donegal buzzes with creativity, boasting a vibrant artistic community showcased in numerous galleries and studios across the county. These venues exhibit a diverse range of styles and mediums, from paintings and sculptures to ceramics, textiles, and jewellery. Many artists even welcome visitors into their working studios, providing a glimpse into the artistic process. Operating hours for galleries and studios vary, so it's best to check their websites or social media for the latest details.

Antiques and Vintage Stores

For those drawn to the allure of the past, Donegal offers a treasure trove of antique shops and vintage stores. Here, you can uncover hidden gems like antique furniture, vintage clothing, collectibles, and unique artefacts steeped in history. Opening hours for these establishments can vary, so it's wise to call ahead or check online listings.

Locations and Recommendations

1. Donegal Town: Wander through galleries and antique shops around the Diamond and High Street, and don't miss the Donegal Craft Shop for local crafts and artwork.

2. Letterkenny: Explore An Grianán Theatre, often hosting art exhibitions alongside its performances.

3. Inishowen: Immerse yourself in the vibrant artistic scene of Inishowen, with galleries and studios dotted across the peninsula.

4. West Donegal: Seek out hidden treasures in antique shops and galleries in towns like Killybegs, Glencolmcille, and Ardara.

Tips for Art and Antique Enthusiasts

1. Many galleries and stores offer shipping options for purchases, especially for larger items.
2. While haggling isn't customary in art galleries, it may be acceptable in some antique shops, particularly for pricier items.
3. Don't forget to inquire about authenticity certificates for valuable antiques.
4. Support local artists and craftspeople by investing in unique souvenirs that embody Donegal's creative essence.

Chapter 9: Planning Your Itinerary

A 7-Day General Itinerary

County Donegal presents a myriad of experiences, from striking cliffs to quaint villages, historical sites, and outdoor pursuits. This proposed 7-day itinerary serves as a foundation to uncover Donegal's highlights, allowing for personalization based on preferences and pacing.

Day 1: Arrival & Donegal Town Exploration

- Commence your journey by arriving at Donegal Airport or driving into the county.
- Settle into your accommodation in Donegal Town.
- Delve into Donegal Town's history by visiting Donegal Castle and the County Museum.
- Stroll through the charming streets, explore the shops at the Diamond, and indulge in a traditional pub lunch.
- In the evening, soak up the lively atmosphere of Donegal Town with some traditional music at a local pub.

Day 2: Slieve League & The Wild Atlantic Way

- Embark on an exhilarating drive along the Wild Atlantic Way toward Slieve

League, boasting Europe's highest accessible sea cliffs.
- Marvel at the awe-inspiring vistas from the viewing platform and venture along the nearby hiking trails.
- Continue your journey along the Wild Atlantic Way, making stops at picturesque villages like Teelin and Bunbeg for scenic walks and fresh seafood.
- Consider unwinding in the hot springs at Harvey's Point Hotel in the evening.

Day 3: Glenveagh National Park and Tory Island

- Devote a day to exploring the majestic Glenveagh National Park. Traverse its scenic trails, visit Glenveagh Castle, and keep an eye out for red deer and other wildlife.
- Take a ferry from Bunbeg or Burtonport to Tory Island, steeped in Gaelic culture and renowned for its artistic heritage. Explore the island's unique landscape, visit the Tory Island Centre, and observe traditional sweater-making.
- Reflect on the day's adventures upon returning to your mainland accommodation.

Day 4: Inishowen Peninsula & Surfing

- Venture north to explore the Inishowen Peninsula, famed for its rugged coastline, sandy beaches, and vibrant artistic community.
- Learn about the 19th-century famine at Doagh Famine Village, hike to Malin Head for panoramic views, and indulge in surfing, if you're feeling adventurous.
- Retreat to a cosy B&B or guesthouse in Inishowen for the night.

Day 5: Discovering Letterkenny & Hiking Trails

- Travel east to Letterkenny, Donegal's largest town. Visit An Grianán Theatre, browse local shops, and embark on a scenic hike in the surrounding hills, perhaps to Sliabh Sneacht for breathtaking views.
- Savour a delectable meal at one of Letterkenny's eateries or pubs in the evening.

Day 6: Ards Forest Park & Hidden Gems

- Head south to Ardara, renowned for its traditional music scene.
- Explore the varied landscapes of Ards Forest Park, hike scenic trails, and uncover remnants of ancient settlements.
- Continue south, stopping at hidden gems like Glencolmcille Folk Village or the Slieve League Coastal Walk.
- Spend the night enjoying live music at a traditional Irish pub in a village like Kilcar or Carrick.

Day 7: Farewell & Final Explorations

- Depending on your departure time, indulge in some last-minute shopping for souvenirs or visit one final attraction.
- Reflect on your unforgettable journey through County Donegal, filled with captivating landscapes, rich history, and vibrant culture.
- Depart from Donegal Airport or venture onward to other destinations as your Irish adventure draws to a close.

Customization Tips

1. This itinerary serves as a guide; tailor it to suit your interests and time

constraints.
2. Consider extending your stay to delve deeper into specific regions.
3. Research local festivals and events to enhance your experience.
4. Book accommodations and tours in advance, especially during peak seasons.

* * *

A 3-Day Romantic Itinerary for Couples

Donegal's stunning landscapes, quaint towns, and rich cultural offerings make it an ideal setting for a romantic escape. Here's a suggested 3-day itinerary designed to rekindle romance and create unforgettable memories for you and your loved one:

Day 1: Discover the Wild Atlantic Way and Savour Local Delights

- Morning: Start in the charming town of Donegal Town. Wander the historic streets, visit Donegal Castle, and take a stroll along the picturesque harbour.

- Lunch: Enjoy a delicious seafood lunch at a waterfront restaurant, savouring fresh catches and stunning views.

- Afternoon: Embark on an exciting cliff coast cruise along the Slieve League cliffs. Marvel at the dramatic scenery and spot nesting seabirds as you hold hands and take in the awe-inspiring views.

- Evening: Check into your romantic accommodation in the Glencolmcille area. Enjoy a traditional Irish dinner in a cosy pub with live music, creating a warm and inviting atmosphere.

Day 2: Explore Hidden Gems and Unleash Your Adventurous Spirit

- Morning: Visit the Glencolmcille Folk Village to learn about Donegal's rich heritage and traditional way of life. Admire the beauty of thatched-roof cottages and local crafts.

- Afternoon: Hike hand-in-hand through the scenic trails of Glenveagh National Park. Enjoy the tranquillity of the woodlands, explore the majestic Poisoned Glen, and admire Glenveagh Castle.

- Optional Activity: For a touch of excitement, try kayaking on Lough Veagh, surrounded by breathtaking mountain scenery.

- Evening: Unwind with a luxurious spa treatment or a relaxing soak in a hot tub at your hotel. Later, enjoy a candlelit dinner with breathtaking views, celebrating your connection and the beauty of Donegal.

Day 3: Discover Inishowen's Charm and Embrace Local Culture

- Morning: Take a scenic ferry ride from Burtonport to Inishowen, a peninsula known for its rugged beauty and artistic spirit.

- Afternoon: Explore the vibrant town of Doagh, visiting the Doagh Famine Village to learn about Ireland's tragic past. Browse local craft shops for unique souvenirs handmade by local artisans.

- Optional Activity: Visit Malin Head, the northernmost tip of Ireland. Stand together at the edge of the world, feeling the power of the wild Atlantic Ocean and the vast horizon.

- Evening: Enjoy a farewell dinner in a traditional pub in Inishowen, soaking up the lively atmosphere on your last night.

Personalise Your Itinerary

1. Adjust the itinerary to fit your interests and preferences.
2. Check for local festivals and events during your stay to add a cultural touch.
3. Consider adding activities like horseback riding on the beach, attending a traditional Irish dance performance, or indulging in a whiskey tasting experience.
4. Embrace Donegal's slow pace. Take long walks, enjoy cosy evenings by the fireplace, and reconnect amidst the beauty of the Irish countryside.

CHAPTER 9: PLANNING YOUR ITINERARY

* * *

A 5-Day Culinary Itinerary

Embark on a delectable journey through County Donegal with this 5-day itinerary designed to immerse you in the region's distinct flavours and culinary heritage. From fresh seafood to hearty stews and unique local dishes, prepare to delight your taste buds and experience Donegal's renowned hospitality.

Day 1: Donegal Town and Surroundings

- Morning: Begin with a traditional Irish breakfast at a quaint cafe in Donegal Town, featuring soda bread, sausages, bacon, and eggs, accompanied by strong Irish tea or coffee.

- Lunch: Visit the Donegal Farmers Market (Saturdays) to sample local produce like fresh cheeses, artisan breads, smoked salmon, and seasonal vegetables. Enjoy a picnic at nearby Lough Eske.

- Dinner: Dine at a waterfront restaurant in Donegal Town, savouring freshly caught fish and chips, creamy seafood chowder, or mussels in white wine and herbs.

Day 2: Wild Atlantic Way Drive and Glencolmcille

- Breakfast: Start your drive along the Wild Atlantic Way with a hearty breakfast at your hotel or B&B, perhaps pancakes with local berries or a porcini mushroom omelette.

- Lunch: Stop for a pub lunch in a village en route, choosing between traditional Irish stew or a smoked salmon and brown bread sandwich.

- Dinner: In Glencolmcille, enjoy a traditional meal at a local guest house or pub, with dishes like Colcannon (mashed potatoes with kale and scallions) and fresh-baked brown bread.

Day 3: Slieve League (Sliabh Liag) and South West Donegal

- Breakfast: Have a substantial breakfast in Glencolmcille, such as kippers or a full Irish breakfast, before hiking.

- Lunch: Pack a picnic with local treats from Glencolmcille, including soda bread, cheeses, and fruit for your hike to the Slieve League cliffs.

- Dinner: After your hike, relax at a pub in Teelin or Kincaslagh, enjoying a Seafood Platter or a pint of Guinness with traditional Irish music.

Day 4: Inishowen Peninsula and Seafood Delights

- Breakfast: Enjoy a leisurely breakfast at your hotel or B&B, such as homemade scones with local jam or a breakfast roll with Irish sausage.

- Lunch: Take a ferry to Inishowen and dine at a seafood restaurant in Greencastle or Moville, with options like lobster thermidor, seared scallops, or seafood linguine.

- Dinner: Explore the lively pub scene in Inishowen, sampling local craft beer and traditional dishes like Drisheen (black pudding).

Day 5: Letterkenny and Local Delicacies

- Breakfast: Have a final Irish breakfast, perhaps oatmeal with fruit and nuts or a breakfast wrap with scrambled eggs and sausage.

- Lunch: On your way out of Donegal, stop in Letterkenny for lunch, trying a Pastie (savoury pastry) or a Gurteen (potato cake with cheese or vegetables).

- Farewell Dinner (Optional): If time permits, enjoy a farewell dinner at a fine-dining restaurant in Letterkenny, featuring modern Irish cuisine with fresh, seasonal ingredients.

Additional Tips

1. Consider booking reservations for popular restaurants, especially during peak season.
2. Be adventurous with trying new dishes.
3. Ask locals for hidden culinary gems and traditional pubs.
4. Enjoy the relaxed pace of your culinary adventure.

Chapter 10: Practical Information and Tips

Language and Communication

Donegal is known for its rich linguistic heritage, featuring a lively Irish-speaking community and a distinctive English dialect. This guide will help you communicate effectively and immerse yourself in Donegal's cultural tapestry:

The Irish Language (Gaeilge)

- Irish, or Gaeilge, is one of Ireland's official languages and is integral to Donegal's cultural identity.

- The Gaeltacht, or Irish-speaking regions, are primarily in West Donegal, especially in places like Glencolmcille and Teelin.

- While fluency in Irish is less common outside the Gaeltacht, using basic phrases such as "Dia dhuit" (Hello) and "Go raibh maith agat" (Thank you) shows respect and appreciation.

Donegal English Dialect

- The English spoken in Donegal has a unique flavour, influenced by Gaelic and a rich oral tradition.

- You may notice unique pronunciations, vocabulary, and sentence structures not found in standard English.

- Examples include:
- "Wee" (small) – "Would you like a wee bit of cake?"
- "Fierce" (very) – "It's fierce cold today!"
- "Craic" (fun) – "We had great craic at the pub last night!"

Communication Tips

1. Don't hesitate to ask for clarification if you don't understand something; most people will gladly explain or rephrase.
2. A smile and friendly demeanour are always appreciated. Locals value visitors who make an effort to communicate.
3. Learning a few basic Irish phrases can be a meaningful gesture and an excellent conversation starter.
4. Embrace the local dialect! It adds to Donegal's charm and character.

Additional Resources

1. Consider downloading a basic Irish phrasebook or a language learning app.

2. Online resources can help you learn basic phrases in Donegal Irish.
3. Local tourist information centres might offer resources or have staff who can answer questions about the language and culture.

* * *

Currency and Money Matters

When exploring the beauty and culture of County Donegal, managing your finances is crucial for a smooth and stress-free experience. Here's a comprehensive guide on currency, using credit and debit cards, tipping etiquette, and other money matters:

Currency

- Euro (€): The official currency of Ireland is the Euro. If you're coming from another European Union country, there's no need to exchange currency.

- Currency Exchange: Visitors from outside the Eurozone can exchange their money for Euros at banks, airports, or currency exchange bureaus.

- ATMs: Automated Teller Machines are widely available throughout Donegal, dispensing Euros and accepting major international debit and credit cards.

Using Credit and Debit Cards

1. Accepted Cards: Major credit cards (Visa, Mastercard) and debit cards with Maestro or Cirrus logos are widely accepted, especially in hotels, restaurants, and larger shops.

2. Carrying Cash: It's wise to carry some cash for smaller purchases in local shops, cafes, or at farmers markets.

3. Notify Your Bank: Before travelling, inform your bank of your travel dates and destination to avoid any issues with card use abroad and to learn about any international transaction fees.

Tipping Etiquette

1. Restaurants: Tipping is not mandatory, but around 10% of the bill is customary if the service charge is not included.
2. Taxis: Rounding up the fare is common practice.
3. Pubs: Tipping is not expected, but you can leave some change for bar staff if they provide excellent service.

Other Money Matters

1. Public Transportation: Many options accept Leap Cards, a prepaid travel card usable on buses and trains throughout Ireland. Consider purchasing one if you plan on extensive use of public transportation.

2. Tax Refunds: Visitors from outside the European Union may be eligible for a Value Added Tax (VAT) refund on purchases. Look for shops displaying the "Tax-Free Shopping" logo and inquire about the refund process.

General Tips

1. Notify Your Bank: To avoid issues with card use abroad, inform your bank of your travel plans.

2. Backup Card: Carry a backup credit or debit card in case your primary card gets lost or stolen.

3. Small Denominations: Keep some Euros in smaller denominations for everyday purchases.

4. Budgeting: Plan your budget according to your travel style and planned activities.

* * *

Health and Safety Tips

Ensuring a safe and healthy trip is crucial for a memorable experience in County Donegal. Here's a comprehensive guide to help you stay safe and healthy throughout your adventure.

General Safety

1. Be Aware of Your Surroundings: Petty theft can happen, so keep valuables secure and avoid carrying large sums of cash.

2. Road Safety: Drive on the left side of the road and be cautious of narrow, winding roads, especially in rural areas. Watch out for sheep and other animals that may wander onto the road.

3. Weather: Donegal's weather can be unpredictable. Pack layers, waterproof gear, and sun protection for all seasons.

4. Emergency Services: Dial 999 for immediate assistance in case of an emergency.

Outdoor Activities

1. Hiking and Walking: Choose trails suitable for your fitness level and experience. Wear appropriate footwear, bring plenty of water, and check weather conditions before heading out. Be cautious of cliffs and uneven terrain.

2. Water Safety: The Atlantic Ocean can be unpredictable. Swim only at designated beaches with lifeguards, be aware of strong currents and riptides, and avoid swimming alone or under the influence of alcohol.

3. Boat Tours: Follow instructions from the tour operator and wear appropriate clothing and life jackets as required.

Tick Awareness

Ticks: Ticks are present in grassy and wooded areas. Be aware of tick-borne illnesses like Lyme disease. After spending time outdoors, thoroughly check yourself and your pets for ticks.

General Health

1. Vaccinations: Ensure you are up-to-date on routine vaccinations before travelling to Ireland.
2. Medical Insurance: It's advisable to have travel insurance that covers medical emergencies.
3. Pharmacies: Pharmacies are widely available in towns and villages throughout Donegal.
4. Drinking Water: Tap water is generally safe to drink. However, you may prefer bottled water, especially in rural areas.

Additional Tips

1. First-Aid Kit: Pack a basic first-aid kit with essentials like bandages, antiseptic wipes, and pain relievers.

2. Itinerary: Let someone know your itinerary and estimated return time, especially if you're planning solo adventures in remote areas.

3. Navigation: Download offline maps or purchase a local map to navigate unfamiliar areas, especially if venturing off the beaten path.

4. Respect the Environment: Leave no trace and dispose of litter responsibly.

By following these tips and using common sense, you can ensure a safe and enjoyable exploration of County Donegal. Embrace the adventure, be prepared, and most importantly, have fun.

Conclusion

County Donegal reveals its enchantment in these pages, inviting you on an unforgettable journey. From stunning coastlines and dramatic cliffs to charming towns rich in history and culture, Donegal has something for every traveller.

This guide has uncovered hidden gems and provided insights into the local lifestyle. You've explored majestic landscapes, from the rugged peaks of Slieve League to the golden sands of secluded coves. You've immersed yourself in Donegal's rich heritage, discovering ancient ruins and vibrant festivals celebrating Gaelic traditions.

But beyond the sights, Donegal's true magic lies in the warmth of its people. The friendly smiles, lively music sessions, and welcoming spirit all contribute to an unforgettable experience.

Whether you seek outdoor adventure, cultural immersion, or simply a chance to relax and reconnect with nature, Donegal offers a haven for the soul. This book has equipped you with the knowledge and inspiration to plan your dream trip.

So, pack your bags, embrace the spirit of adventure, and prepare to discover the magic of County Donegal. Explore hidden beaches, hike through stunning landscapes, and savour the region's unique flavors. Let Donegal cast its spell on you, creating memories that will last a lifetime.

Printed in Dunstable, United Kingdom